ALL MIRACLE

Gift Wrapped

April 9, 1924–February 16, 1999

ALL MIRACLE

Gift Wrapped

Poems by
Elizabeth B. Rooney

Edited by
Patricia M. Rooney

Brigham Farm Publishing

Published by Brigham Farm Publishing
2990 Cave of the Mounds Road
Blue Mounds, WI 53517
www.brighamfarm.com

Cover artwork is from an oil painting by Steven R. Kozar titled "Winter Solitude" © 2001 Steven R. Kozar. For more information about paintings and prints by this artist, check www.stevenkozar.com.

Interior artwork © 2001 Simone Portia McLoughlin

Cover and book design by Elizabeth Ragsdale

Quote by Luci Shaw in preface is used with permission of the author.

Library of Congress Control Number: 2001119947

ISBN 0-9716001-0-4 (set of four)
ISBN 0-9716001-1-2 (v. 1)
ISBN 0-9716001-2-0 (v. 2)
ISBN 0-9716001-3-9 (v. 3)
ISBN 0-9716001-4-7 (v. 4)

To Pat, Norma, Sharol,
Joyce, Kristin, and Eugenia.
These books wouldn't be here
without your love and support.

ALL MIRACLE SERIES

Elizabeth B. Rooney

Morning Song

Packages

Storing September

Gift Wrapped

Contents

December

January

February

Preface

This series of books is for all of Elizabeth Rooney's family, friends and fans who have been patiently awaiting the publication of her collected poems and for all those who will meet her for the first time in these pages.

Elizabeth Brigham Rooney, my mother, began writing poems in the summer of 1978. Before her death in February 1999, she had written over seven hundred of them, interspersed amongst the prose entries in her journals like bursts of song.

She was more surprised than anyone at this sudden and abundant release of creativity, although she'd been encouraged from her youth to pursue a career in writing. Raised by highly literate parents, she attended and excelled at top-notch schools, yet protested, "I don't have anything to say!"

Later, she came to realize the creative flow had been blocked, among other things, by fear of failing those who expected so much from her. It wasn't until she made a complete surrender to the One who had placed the love of poetry inside her that she was free, not only to write but also to embrace all of life as a holy gift.

This "total commitment," as she described it, came as she was preparing to be inducted into the Society of the Companions of the Holy Cross, a lay order of Episcopal women. She already had her masters in Christian Education and was married to an Episcopal priest, yet there was something missing.

"For years I'd been an active Christian adult and before that, a rather timid, but believing child. I prayed quite regularly for as long as I can remember, but at the same time stayed a safe distance from the cross. To embrace the cross wholeheartedly requires an act of will. To my astonishment, the result was an absolute flooding of joy. I had fallen in love with God. It was as if my veins were bubbling with champagne and the poems began to flow freely, coming as delightful surprises day after day."

The first one to come was "Adelynrood," named for the retreat center in Massachusetts where the encounter took place.

Adelynrood

The winter of my heart
Melts here.
Rivulets run
Beneath the ice of fear.

Pierced by your warmth,
Life moves.
Spring has begun.
I feel the sun, the sun!

8/11/78

As her newly awakened faith grew, so did the conviction that these poems were gifts to be shared. She summoned the courage to exchange poetry with friends who were fellow writers. Then she attended a workshop led by the poet Luci Shaw and there found a kindred heart and mind, a friend and mentor, who eventually introduced her to the reading public in a way Elizabeth never dreamed possible.

Luci had been asked to write a chapter in an upcoming book entitled *Bright Legacy, Portraits of Ten Outstanding Christian Women* about someone she "particularly admired." As Luci explains in her chapter, "Rather then telling of the impact on my life of an internationally known personality, I felt a growing conviction that I would rather talk about someone like Elizabeth Rooney, an 'ordinary' woman, hardly known beyond her own circle of friends and colleagues, though uniquely gifted by God. Her experience would, I was sure, suggest to other women with earthbound, unremarkable lives that he could lift the most mundane existence into his own bright beauty and glory. What he requires are eyes open to his brightness and ears alert for his voice."

Luci's words so aptly describe the gift Elizabeth received at Adelynrood. She had indeed been given "eyes open to his brightness and ears alert for his voice." And so the woman who had protested she had nothing to write about, was able to declare, "I know what I want to say. . . . I want to write about God, about the intense tenderness manifest in the world wherever goodness, truth and beauty allow it to shine through… Today in the parking lot there was a puddle—a muddy, shallow puddle on the blacktop, not more than an inch deep at best and perhaps four feet across. When looked at from a certain angle, it reflected all the treetops in it, and clouds and sky, all the way to infinity. I think I'm like the puddle—muddy, shallow, insignificant—but, by God's grace, capable of the miracle of reflecting him, and in him, all the wonder of the universe.

"The more I become aware of the active presence of God, the more beautiful and sacred everything becomes. . . . Do we need miracles, or do we need only to perceive that every ordinary thing around us is already miraculous?"

My mother's hope, as voiced in the following prayer by an unknown author, was that her poems might open other eyes to His brightness and other ears to His voice, that they would come to understand as she had that "Life is *all* miracle."

"Days pass and the years vanish and we walk sightless among miracles. Lord, fill our eyes with seeing and our minds with knowing. Let there be moments when your Presence, like lightning, illumines the darkness in which we walk. Help us to see, wherever we gaze, that the bush burns unconsumed. And we, clay touched by God, will reach out for holiness and exclaim in wonder, 'How filled with awe is this place and we did not know it.'"

《 》

This series, *All Miracle*, includes four volumes, *Morning Song, Packages, Storing September,* and *Gift Wrapped,* which correspond to spring, summer, autumn, and winter. Those who, like my mother, have grown up on farms or in the country understand and interpret life, in large part, by the passage of the seasons. Her poetry is characterized by a deep awareness of life's interconnectedness and the yearly cycles of death and rebirth. After much reading and rereading of the poems, I felt the most natural way to group them would be by these intrinsic themes, which include not only the four seasons but also the parallel seasons of human life, such as childhood, adulthood, aging, and death and the corresponding seasons of the liturgical year, such as Advent, Christmas, Lent, and Easter. Although each poem is meant to be read and savored on its own, the groupings are intended to accentuate their collective rhythm and flow.

—*Patricia M. Rooney*

Acknowledgments

My most sincere thanks to the following persons and companies:

To all who helped launch this publishing venture by generously contributing to the Elizabeth B. Rooney Memorial Poetry Fund.

To Eugenia Brown, who so cheerfully volunteered hours and hours of typing.

To Louise Summers, Delores Topliff, Pat Hitchcock, Norma Madsen, Sharol Hayner, Joyce Young, Kimberly Linyard, Janice Griffin, and Sr. Peronne-Marie Thiebert, for their gracious help with proofreading.

To my brother Mark, for all of his encouragement, advice, and nagging.

To the wonderful folks at Impressions Book and Journal Services, Inc., especially John Ferguson, Mary Boss, and Elizabeth Ragsdale, for their expertise, enthusiasm, and genuine interest in this project. Your patience and warmth working with a first-time publisher made all the difference.

To Kevin Wasowski and Jane Landen of Edwards Brothers, for their kind and professional help.

Winter

This week's *New Yorker* has a cartoon of a couple standing in a room cluttered with Christmas—decorations and newly opened presents. The husband is saying, "Well, that's that. Onto 1982!" I feel a little like that, yet I'm reluctant to have Christmas be turned off and picked up and put away. I do not want to put away the crèche, to leave the stable, to go back to acting as though You were not the most important thing in the universe, the Center of all that is, the Reason for my being and the Delight of my dailyness.

Journal, 12/26/81

Gift Wrapped

When God was wrapping up the universe
He chose star-studded tissue for the sky,
A flowered-green for earth,
And blue foil shot with silver
For the sea.
He gave us everything—
Even Himself, the perfect gift of Love.
Surprising gift—
A baby wrapped in swaddling clothes,
Lying on straw.

12/9/93

December

Quiet Time

Now are we winter deep
In quietness.
The shadowed snow,
The gliding owl,
The moon
Keep silent vigil now.

We can be still,
So still we start to know
The depth of everything,
So still we hear the stars
Begin to sing.

1/5/82

Investment

Gold plummets from the sky
As finches fall
Out of the winter oak tree
By the feeder.

Gold pierces westward
From the rising sun
Burnishing finch and feeder
As it comes.

Fool's gold,
Intangible and bright,
To hoard within my heart
Against the night.

4/10/82

Dry Grass

I would be sere
And brown and barren
Now,
The urgency of spring
Withdrawn,
Invisible to me.
I would be deeply quiet
Resting here
Beneath the gathering snow.

There is no effort left in me,
Only the slow, still resting
And the waiting for the spring.
It is a good time, this—
This time of quietness,
This time of letting go
Of everything.

12/7/86

Hibernating

Now as the creeping cold
Drives all my vital forces
Toward their core,
I feel the need
To gather comfort round me,
Bar the door
And spend the winter
Dreaming of the spring.

This time of year,
I envy chuck and bear.
Would my fur were as thick as theirs
And that I had some lair
Deep in the sheltering earth
Where I could keep
All of my fears and foes at bay
And sleep.

10/16/84

Night

Night should be
Dark enough
For stars
And still enough
For prayer—

A time to see
What we cannot see
By day,
A time to know
What we will never know
Unless we pray.

7/14/86

Stars

Swallow a skyful of stars!
Then, close your eyes
And taste their mystery.
Feel in yourself
The cold immensity
Of all the space that lies
Among, between, around
That far, faint light.
Taste all the shining frostiness
Of night!

12/6/88

Rediscovery

The winter skies
Sparkle
With more than frost.
Magic the ancients knew
And we have lost
Lies there
Among the stars.

Will we again
Learn to stand still
In the enclosing dark?
Hush now and hark!

12/6/88

Annunciation

There was
Is
Has been
And will be
An everywhere
Fixed
And transfixed
Within
That point in time
Wherein
One single
Simple
Open soul
Received
The potency
Of the creative whole.

7/28/80

Joseph

Joseph was a good man.
It's hard to be a good man here below.
Joseph was true, true as a tree is true.
Joseph did what the angel told him to do.
When Mary needed his shelter, he was there,
Strong as a tree, four square.
Joseph knew how to obey.
We'd call him Joe if he were living today . . .
"Hey, Joe, can you mend my hay rack?"
"Why, Joe, you've done a beautiful job on my chair!"
Yes, Joseph was a good man.
When God needed him, he was there.

12/24/78

Christmas Shopping

Somewhere between the ornaments
And the electric toys,
The Child was lost.
Perhaps it was the noise,
Perhaps the cost
Of Christmas gifts these days,
Perhaps the maze of counters
And the gaze
Of faces lost to love
Beneath the glaze of weariness.

He was right next to me for a while.
I remember His sweetness, His smile.
Perhaps I turned up the wrong aisle.
I am, I suppose, looking for Bethlehem
Here on the second floor.
Is this the place to look?
Or will the clerk be telling me
That they don't carry holy mystery
In this department any more?

12/21/80

Customs

The English gave us Yule logs,
The high-hung mistletoe.
The Germans brought the Christmas tree
In from the cold and snow.

The Swedish praise St. Lucia
And set a sheaf of wheat
High on a pole above the snow
So winter birds can eat.

The Dutch gave us St. Nicholas,
And Clement Clarke Moore
Added all the reindeer
And the sleigh outside our door.

Norwegians have krummkakken
And special Christmas treats,
While Christmas songs from every land
Are caroled in our streets.

But so that we'd remember
The God who came in flesh
And worship Him at Christmastime,
St. Francis made the créche.

11/25/81

Ingathering

Starshine is all our light.
The saddles creak
And the night flows past
The swiftly moving thighs
And the silent hooves.
We are kings riding, riding
To where a babe is hiding.

The donkey moves with my hand.
Faithful in spite of fatigue,
He carries Mary
Who carries the hope of the world.
We are young, anxious and proud,
Anonymous in the crowd
Going toward Bethlehem.

The sound of bells and of bleating
Tells us the flock
Is stirring within the rock-strewn
Barrenness of this land.
We are rough men used to the night—
What is that music, that light?

Father God, Lover of Men,
Watching the cave and the kings,
The innkeeper summoned from sleep,
The shepherds, the sheep,
Hearing the angel song swelling,
You know, as none of us know,
The Glory this moment is telling.

11/25/79

Housekeeper

This is my little town,
My Bethlehem,
And here, if anywhere,
My Christ Child
Will be born.

I must begin
To go about my day—
Sweep out the inn,
Get fresh hay for the manger
And be sure
To leave my heart ajar
In case there may be travelers
From afar.

12/9/78

Shepherds

We sleep in peace
And wake to blessedness,
To find the glory of the Lord
Shining around us.
The music fills our hearts
And overwhelms our minds.
We grope for wakefulness
And for one perfect lamb
To offer
To the baby named I AM.

12/11/78

Star Song

There had been stars
Year after desert year,
A cold light
And a distant
For stars are never near.

Until the light
That lighted all the world
Consented to be born.

The night He came
The stars swung low
And sang
As morning stars had sung
Creation's morn.

So sing we now.
Star-crossed,
We sing the bright
And morning star
Shining among us,
Banishing our night.

12/13/82

Confrontation

The soldiers pause
And, wondering, stand
Upon the dark Arabian sand.
Is that sound music, voices, song
Or have they just been listening to the wind
Too long?
Some even know
The old miraculous story
Of how the angels came
In clouds of glory.
But no one believes in angels
Any longer.
They can't be real.
Still, as the music and the light
Grow stronger,
Some of the soldiers kneel.

12/12/90

Respite

The whole world stops for Christmas.
Distracted, anxious, overworked,
We pause,
Find our attention caught and held
By a child's smile.

For a day, for a moment,
We forget our plans to destroy each other
Either globally
Or within the intimate bitterness
Of our so-called homes.

The child
Smiles . . .
And the shells
Of all our selves
Creak and begin to crack
As we smile back.

12/26/79

Rumor

They say it's only a Christmas fable
That just at Midnight out in the stable
Amid the darkness and fragrant hay
The animals drop to their knees to pray.

I've never seen them. I don't know how
You would find every horse, every sheep, every cow
Suddenly kneeling there in the straw
God-struck with the wonder of Christmas, the awe.

But I've heard it said that on Christmas night
When the snow is shining and stars are bright,
The animals kneel because they remember
The ox and the ass in that first December.

11/25/81

Christmas

Star shine
And love
Come
From above.

Angels
And singing,
Shepherds
Gifts bringing.

Camels
And kings
Carrying
Things.

Stables
And inns,
New life
Begins.

Jesus
His name,
Softly
Love came.

12/12/82

God Incarnate

You were a babe
And a young girl held you, singing,
Called you her sweeting,
Her dearling, her lovey, her best,
Cradled you tenderly,
Cuddled you close on her breast.
You were a babe
And a young girl held you, singing.

You were a babe
And a young girl held you, singing.
Tender you were as the new green springing,
Fragile as blossom, beautiful as the sun.
And Mary called you her darling,
Her sweet lamb, her dearest,
Her poppet, her precious, her treasure,
Her own little one.
You were a babe
And a young girl held you, singing.

1/25/87

Cradle Song

Born in a stable
And laid in the hay,
God's gift of love to us
Ever and aye—
Sweet baby Jesus.

Tiny and vulnerable,
Yet unafraid,
Lord of the world
In the world that He made—
Sweet baby Jesus.

Trusting Himself
To the goodness of man,
Shelter Him, Joseph,
However you can—
Sweet baby Jesus.

Sleeping and nursing
So fragile, so tender,
Here in our flesh,
The omnipotent splendor—
Sweet baby Jesus.

12/25/78

God Given

Christmas means gifts.
In the wide, wheeling universe
There has been only one—
One gift once given,
One infinite, eternal, perfect joy—
One baby boy.

12/7/78

Christmas Present

God was looking for a carpenter.
He wanted a skilled craftsman
To make Him a cross.
The wood must be hard and wide,
Straight cut with the joints perfectly squared
And planed as smooth as a yoke.
Finally, he needed a handful of nails
And then, God hung the perfect gift
Upon the perfect tree—
Love, present with us through eternity.

12/12/78

Presence

They named Him
With the meaning of His message.
Immanuel
Rings like a bell.
It sounds the knell of sinning,
Of all that we have sinned
Since the beginning.

They named Him
With His message—
God is here.
God with us, with us, with us
Year by year,
With everyone
In every everywhere.

We cannot sleep or work
Or fantasize
Or hide in work or play
Hoping in vain
That God will go away.

The Maker of the world
Is with us in it.
Immanuel is here,
Right here, this minute.

6/9/79

Child

Dear child, sweet child,
Sleeping in the straw,
We who come to worship you
Kneel now in awe.

Dear child, sweet child,
Sheltered in a stable,
Each of us would bring you
Gifts, as we are able

Dear child, sweet child,
Lighted by a star,
Help our hearts to find you,
No matter where we are.

Dear child, sweet child,
Willing to be a man,
Teach us how to love you;
No one else can.

12/16/81

Lullaby for a Christian

Sleep sweetly child,
The arms of Love
Enfold you,
Rest now, be still,
Relax
And let Him hold you.
The day was His,
And now
His is the night,
And you, entirely His,
All will come right.
Entrust yourself to Him,
Whose love has bound you.
Sleep sweetly, child,
And let His love surround you.

11/11/86

Mary's Song

I have hidden you well
These nine months long,
Little one, little one.

But tonight the sky
Is alive with song,
Little one, little one.

I see kings kneel
By your manger bed,
Little one, little one.

But other kings
Will wish you dead,
Little one, little one.

God find you refuge,
Find you friend,
Little one, little one.

For what's begun
Can never end,
Little one, little one.

12/12/82

Rich Man

Rich man, rich man,
Who are you?
Do you seek the Christ Child, too?

In your palace and your court
Life is busy, life is short.
Have you time to go away
To find a Baby in the hay?

Can you get your camel through
The needle's eye,
As you must do?

Rich man, rich man,
You've come far.
Where did you learn to trust a star,
Instead of turning to a king
To guide you in your wandering?

Rich man, how did you get wise
In spite of all your kingly guise?
Who taught you to play your part,
To bring an educated heart
To the stable in the west
So you could kneel there and be blest?

12/23/78

Gifts

What shall I bring You,
King, my king,
Creator and giver of everything?
What shall I bring?

Shall I bring You the work of my hands,
The gold
Of all of the years of my growing old?
Shall I bring You gold?

Shall I bring You prayer,
The long intense
Hours when silence grows immense,
When the spirit ascends like frankincense?
Shall I bring You prayer?

Shall I bring You myrrh,
The suffering with,
The learning to let each other live,
To care and to share and still forgive?
Shall I bring You myrrh?

What shall I bring You,
King, my king?
The love in my heart,
The songs I sing,
The will to obey You in everything.
These will I bring, O king, my king!

12/11/82

Slaughter of the Innocents

There will be blood on the snow
Beneath the Christmas moon.
Gather the child and go.
Go soon!

Carry him safe to Egypt,
The child who came to save,
For the little boys of Bethlehem
Will soon lie in their grave.

There will be weeping in the streets
Beneath the winter sky.
Since Herod fears the holy child,
The Jewish child must die.

The child of peace is sleeping
On the Egyptian sands;
The sword he brought is reeking
In Herod's soldiers' hands.

Oh, child, who came to bring us
Good tidings and great joys,
The families of Bethlehem
Are weeping for their boys!

11/29/81

Bethlehem Revisited

Welcome, my Lord!
You are indeed
Well come.
Won't you step in?
We do not bustle
As we once did, Lord.
The times have passed us by.
The children all are grown
And they relocated the road.
Not many people find us now . . .
How did you happen by?
You say that you remember us, my Lord,
That you were here once long ago
And have come back
To see the place your family told you of?
It's strange I don't recall
Anyone quite so regal.
There was one winter when we saw a star
And there were kings once
Who had come from far,
But I don't think they had a child . . .
And you say you were very small?
That's how it is in this business, my Lord.
People come and I try to be kind,
But they go away so soon again.
Nobody really sticks in my mind.

2/5/79

New Year's Eve

I feel the exquisite edge of the present.
Sword-thin, steel sharp,
It pierces those
Who dwell too long upon it.
I peer down toward the past,
But it has vanished;
I teeter forward
Only to find the future lost in mist.
Balancing on this point
Of agony
Amid the stream of time,
I move mechanically
To the music of Guy Lombardo.
Perhaps if I keep jerking up and down,
I will not have to confront
The reality of this
Or any moment.

1/1/79

January

January

This sun-sparkled,
Snow-shining,
Ice-diamond day
Flames
Along every gleaming twig and branch
As winter celebrates
The frozen radiance.

Oh, heart's love,
Let us run and dance and fly
Among the diamond-shining trees
Beneath the ice-blue sky.

1/21/88

Hush

Winter has tucked me in,
Laid her cool finger
Softly on my lips
And whispered, "Hush."
As I grow still,
A thousand, thousand hushes
Fall past my window sill.
Silently,
Each one brushes
Against my eyes
And I grow quiet,
Stilled, and winter wise.

12/28/87

Love's Handiwork

Only a God of love
Would care enough
To make the winter sky
So deep a blue.

Only a God of love
Would glaze each branch with ice,
Then sugar it with frost
So that each shining twig
Reflects light twice.

Only a God of love
Would sculpture snow
In drifts so lavish,
Such a blinding white.

Only a God of love
Would make from cold
This dazzling crystal filigree.
Open your winter-weary eyes
And see!

12/2/85

Snow

The snow comes
Lightly, whitely,
Dancing down.
It seems to play at winter,
Unafraid
Of cold
Or of its own fragility.

We watch a miracle
As all these tiny, exquisite
Bits of creation
Pour down on us
Till the accumulation
Muffles and stills and stops
Our busy nation.

12/30/95

Snow Shower
in Sunshine

The air twinkles.
God is laughing
With joy.

12/26/78

Winter Gift

The forest bloomed last night.
Snow blossoms sprang
Dazzling and pure
From every leaf and bough.
We thought all dead
And now, in a few hours,
Old leaves, dry branches
Show this weight of flowers.
Winter brings its own miracles.
We who have lived them know.
When all seems cold and sad,
God fills the barren wood
With flowers of snow.

1/4/90

Timid

The rabbit kneels in snow.
I, by the window.
We nibble scraps of love—
His, apple,
Mine, self-knowledge.
But both of us lack trust.
He feels the dawn
And hops beneath the woodpile.
And I, who feel awareness,
Freeze
Lest God find me visible.
Later, safe in my interlacing duties,
I peer out
Remembering the sweetness of the gift
Spread on the snow of silent solitude.

12/27/78

Winter Watch

The window's open.
Nothing lies between
God's quiet and my heart.
The winter birds
Whir down to hop about
Among the seeds.
Their movement just accentuates
The stillness
Of the white surrounding air.
I wish I could become
As peaceful as the trees
And as aware.

3/4/89

Trinity

"Three for a fire..."
New England wisdom knows
Its granite certainties.
Sharing its harsh truths
Sparingly,
The voice,
As full of silences as speech,
Recalls the quiet
Of the upland meadows.
A man who knows
Sparse summers and long snows
Must also know
How best to warm
The spirit of the hands.
Aloneness will not do
And even two wear out
Each other's warmth.
True fire takes three—
You and our Lord and me.

10/29/78

Winter Solitude

Tonight, I'm all alone!
Even the backs of the books are closed against me.
The cold has stilled the sibilance of summer.
Silence falls from the clouds.
I could reach out to the radio . . .
Perhaps the phone
Will interrupt this silence and this space.
Help me to cherish quietness,
To crave this gift of peace
In the midst of time.
Teach me to love your stillness, Lord.
Help me to climb the rungs of silence
Till they meet the sky.
I know you wait within the quiet, Lord,
Why, then, am I afraid?

11/28/78

Protected

An icicle of fear
Pierces my heart.
Such sorrow
Need not be.
Icicles melt
When the sun touches them.
Fears melt, too,
When they are brought
To You.

12/26/83 *(St. Stephen's Day)*

For a Traveler in Winter

"Whoso putteth his trust in the Lord shall be safe."
Proverbs 29:25.

Lord, place a shining shield
Around my child.
Tonight,
The snow is deep,
The wind is wild.
I cannot be with her
Except in prayer,
Yet am I comforted
Because I know
That You are there.

2/8/88

Small Voyagers

Small boys, defying gravity and cold,
Speed down the ice,
Bold with success;
They've conquered winter twice.
Red-cheeked, triumphant,
Swift and sure, they sail—
Small ships
Before a windy, freezing gale.

Lord, may they move through life
With equal strength and grace
Whatever tests and trials
They have to face.

2/12/94

Small Teacher

When I found hope and courage
Failing me,
God in His mercy
Sent a chickadee.

This lively little ball
Of merry song
Popped out of nowhere,
Briefly hopped along
The feeder's edge.
Then flew into the wood.

His cheerful trust
Renewed in me
The faith
That God is good.

8/16/92

Foragers

Solemn as judges in a row,
Their black robes trailing in the snow,
Five wary, wise, wild turkeys go.
Pilgrims of winter
In the hungry moon,
For these, like us
Spring cannot come too soon.

2/12/94

Prayer for a Cold Night

Lord, bless your furred and feathered ones
This night.
Shelter them from the bitter cold,
The fight that freezing darkness brings.
Help them to find
Acorns and nuts, suet and seeds
Enough to bind
The warm life in their bodies
Till the sun
Returns with its bright promise
Of spring.

1/15/94

To a Tree in Moonlight

Hand
With ten thousand fingers,
Are you trying
To reach acorns
Buried by the snow?
Do you think the magic
Of the winter moon
Will give you back
Your russet autumn glow?

Hand with ten thousand fingers,
You explore
Within the crystalled cold,
But all is vain.
Only the mystery
Of warmth and spring
Can fill your budded fingers
Once again.

11/19/86

Night Beauty

Cold grips the land.
The winter moon
Draws tracings of each tree
Upon the snow.
And stars!
You never see such stars
Unless the mercury's at ten below
With not one cloud
Between you and the ends of paradise.

12/9/78

Plea

Lord, when my life grows bleak
And bitter cold
And I walk shivering and bare
Across the years and hours of despair,
Help me to see the diamond light
Of your love
Shimmering within my night.

12/9/78

One Dying

It looks so cold out there,
And the light
Only reaches the edge of the woods.
Why must I go?
I'm afraid of the dark
And the snow.

They say that afterwards
It will be warm and beautiful
And light.
I wonder if they really know.
I only wish I didn't have to go
Into the freezing night.

12/1/88

Last Days

The tall, tall candle
Has burned down at last.
Now just a scrap of flame
Floats in a tiny, shrinking
Pool of wax.
The bit of flax
That was a wick
Has disappeared.
We can remember
When he lighted up our lives,
Burned strong and bright.
Now all his shining strength
Lies sputtering low,
Barely alive,
But not yet altogether out;
Not quite

3/15/89

Terminally Ill

Pain mounts
And crashes over me,
And I am sucked,
Despairing,
Down the sands
Of my last days.

The sands run out,
The sands run out,
And I have not the courage left
To ask for stay
Of this slow execution
Of my bones.

People I love
Fade in and out
Of what is left
Of this my life.

I would have liked
Another twenty years;
I dread their tears—
And mine.

I wish I had
More strength
To fight this undertow.
The pain
Begins again . . .
When will I go?

1/15/89 *"Just trying to imagine
what it must be like for dear, brave
Charlie (brother) to go on hurting and
fighting and loving and expecting to die."*

Role Reversal

I shuffled slowly toward my dying day,
But now, transformed by death, I run, I leap.
Clear-eyed and strong, I hurry on my way
Wakened from life as from a heavy sleep.

When I was patient, you were patient, too,
Wearily waiting my recovery.
But now, impatient, I've abandoned you
To take this journey of discovery.

It's hard to time our timing perfectly.
My time has come; your time has not run out.
And I, on whom you waited,
Could not wait that side of death.

Do not be frightened, dear, and do not doubt!
When you come, I will greet you with the joy
We knew when you were girl and I was boy.

10/7/78

Legacy

What can I give Him?
I can give Him you
And my life lived without you,
Bravely, beautifully,
With all the love we knew
Not lost
But redistributed.
Lord, keep me true
To all the best that grew
In each of us
Thanks to our lovely loving.

9/2/89

Parting

When you have learned
Through years of loving living,
To cherish someone's life
More than your own,
It is almost impossible to face
The prospect of a death
That will mean giving
This, your beloved,
Totally to God
And going on alone.

Time heals, they say.
Who knows?
At some far future day,
Perhaps it will.
Now,
Time is just a hard and endless road
Stretching up hill.

We knew, of course,
That someday this would come;
That one of us would stand
Looking upon the dead face of the other.
We did not let the grim prognosis
Smother our joy; we blithely set aside our fears.

There was too much of living
And of laughter,
Of struggle and of fun.
We had no time to think of
What came after,
When one life would go on
While one was done.

Sleep well, my love!
The joy of God enfold you.
Your pain has ended;
My pain has begun.
And yet I know
I am by God befriended
And one brave day
I, too, will see the Son.

11/14/94

Together

Never were you
More perfectly my own,
Nor I more yours,
Than during those last hours
When alone,
Bereft of hope
For health
Or longer life,
We looked together
At the face of death.

Never were you
More husband,
I, more wife
Than when we watched
Together
As your life
Diminished
And ran down.

Death separates,
They say,
Yet love, triumphant,
Bound us each to each.
Facing finality,
We found a closeness
Even death can't breach.

1/29/86

Old Friend

Lie down, old dog.
Find somewhere soft
To comfort your old bones.

I know you find it hard
To see and hear,
Hard to do stairs,
Impossible
To chase and catch a squirrel.

Just settle by the stove
And curl in its warm comfort
As you near your end.
Rest peacefully, old friend.

1/9/90

To a Nun in Danger of Death

From you I borrow courage,
Dear my friend.
I see you face death peacefully,
With trust.
From you, no panic cry
Of, "Lord, You must . . ."
Only the quiet laying down of will,
The being still.

You are as peaceful
As a little child
Going to sleep
Upon its mother's breast.
Because you've given God
Your daily life,
You now know how
To give Him all the rest.

8/10/87

Becoming

Death is a gift of love.
We do not seek the gift,
Would not go gentle into that good night,
And yet, it is in dying we are born.
We live in fear of pain,
Scorn weakness,
Hate disease.
Yet these are means to God's intended end
Of glorifying each of us.
For only when we leave ourselves behind
Can we begin to be.

1/4/79

Old Cat

The cat is dying in the living room.
I move about my ordinary ways—
Eat breakfast, clear the dishes,
Sweep the floor.

I pause from time to time
To stoke her fur,
To listen for her breath,
To gauge the gradual advance of death.

She waits
As still and patient
As if death were mouse or mole
And she were crouched intent
Outside his hole.

An old, old cat,
So frail there is nothing left
Inside her fur
But courage and dignity
And one almost inaudible
Last purr.

9/12/80

Poet's Lament

They keep trying
To get behind the words
And reach me.
Now that I'm dead,
They peer at my picture
And wonder
What it was like
To be the person I was.

Why can't they just accept
The things I said?
"That's who I was—
There in those lines of verse.
I've already told you
And showed you
And spelled it out.
You wouldn't have learned any more
If you'd been there
When I was alive."

A few friends know at once,
But most people strive and strive
To analyze my meaning
And never do arrive.

3/31/88

On the Reconstruction
of Emily Dickinson's Writings

They take their tedious shovels
And excavate her prose.
Her winged words
Lie matted on the page.
If their dear Emily
Were not escaped and free,
How she would rage!

10/10/93

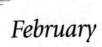

February

New View

Fog simplifies.
It wipes away the distant fields,
The hills,
The sun and moon and stars,
The lights of town.
Gently, but totally,
It closes down
All those distractions
That keep me from seeing
The beauty in the present
And the near.
Fog makes me look anew
And find for the first time
The loveliness
That's always been right here.

12/28/91

Heightened Perception

I would not want
To have my last day be
One I had failed to live.

You who have given life
And so much love to me,
How can I ever thank You
That You give
This final gift of poignancy?

Suddenly, all the sweets
I've ever known
Are sweeter, more intense,
And my small world, immense
With the significance of life.

Curious,
How the very death we fear
Illuminates the near!

8/24/87

Emancipation

Once you have met
And have accepted
Death,
You find surprisingly
That you've been freed
To live.

The willingness to die
Not just eventually
But today,
If God so wills,
Involves
A giving of yourself away.

That done,
You're free
To be.

1/19/88

Release

Pale rider, have you come for me at last?
You took my Indian pony long ago.
The years between have been so slow, so slow . . .
Once I rode free.
Nothing between my Indian horse and me,
We fled like wind
Across the open plain.

They sent me away to school
And tried to contain
The headstrong wildness of me.
Years, all those years,
Of teaching and lonely meals
And embroidery
And finally, T.V.
They tried.
In a way they won,
Except that the fires within me
Never died.

So you have come at last
To take me to ride
Over the edge of the world.
Because they dread you and your horse,
Pale Rider,
They will not see
The sudden surging happiness in me
At last to ride again
And to ride free.

3/17/81

Emancipated

Carl died last night,
Died at eleven o'clock
In his hospital bed,
Escaped quite suddenly
From needles and tubes
And procedures
And blinking machines.

It must have felt so good
To be awake and alive
And able to love
Without any shadow of illness
Or possibility of death—
A miracle achieved
By drawing his last breath.

7/14/87

Death

Death is the final blessing
Of this life.
The darkened glass
Will thin,
Become a sheet of smoke
And, suddenly,
We'll stand
In front of perfect Love.
He will hold out His arms
And we will run
Into their shelter
Safely home at last.

5/11/86

Widow

Standing before the window,
Missing Joe,
She watches falling snow.
So much of her life's buried,
Like the leaves.
Let the snow come and come
And pile up drifts
Until they reach the eaves!
What does it matter now?
What can she do with spring
When spring does come?
Better to live in winter,
Cold and numb.

2/12/94

Letting Go

Day dies.
The brightness dims.
The glow is fading
From the western sky.
It was a lovely day—
Sun-warmed, snow-bright,
Alive with birds and squirrels.
I hate to lose it
In the coming night.
I want to hold day close,
To cling
And say that I will not forget,
To bring this day alive again . . .
And yet,
If I stay shut within my memories
And nourish sorrow,
I will miss all the wonder
Of tomorrow.

For Those Who Mourn

Celebrate!
Celebrate me!
The shell you see
Was useful,
Served me well,
Gave me great pleasure even,
But it was a shell
And so, wore out
And had to be discarded
In the end.
But I,
Who animated it,
I did not die.
I am new born and free.
Celebrate!
Celebrate me!

3/3/88

For Those We Love

Grant them
The green glory of heaven,
Of morning that grows
In ever-expanding joy.

Grant them
The swiftness and grace
Of love that outruns
The farthest reaches of space.

Grant them light
Shining through every cell,
Revealing, forgiving all,
Making all well.

Grant that they may discover
And rediscover
The deepest depths of Your love,
Oh, heavenly Lover.

12/9/79

Anticipation

Does death, then, come like dawn—
The high clouds turning pearl,
The birds beginning to shout joy,
A rising breeze,
And suddenly,
Light breaking through the trees?

2/8/79

Complete

When all my songs
Have stuttered into silence
And I stand awed and stilled,
Tongue-tied and thrilled
By majesty and glory,
Then it will be enough
To know Your Presence,
Enough simply to be
One small, responsive
Part of Your creation
Known as me.

6/19/94

Practice of the Presence

The brightness burns
Along the brittle bone.
Heart-haunted,
I am jolted by the thud
Of Love along my veins.
Flesh turns translucent.
Mind, abashed,
Resigns its tyranny.
And only God remains!

8/17/78

Depths

I would sink
Silently
Into the stillness
Of God.
I would drop down,
Down like a stone
Into the limitless
Depths
Of His love.

Since He is infinite,
I might just
Keep on falling,
Falling ever more deeply
In love
Forever.

1/9/86

Ocean

Oh, I am fathoms deep
In love with Love.
The shell of me
Lies on the ocean floor
Sunk, flooded, overwhelmed
By the tide of joy.
I am only dimly aware
Of the sands
Above and around me.
Grace has found me.

8/6/79

Who I Am

Distilled by stillness,
All my thoughts evaporate
And leave
Only their essence
Potent, crystallized,
Waiting to be distilled
In words.
Perhaps there's one word
That contains
All I have learned and am.
The word is "yours"
Just "yours," Lord Jesus,
"Yours."

4/30/94

Valentines

The world's a valentine from God,
More intricate than lace,
Sweeter than roses,
Fragrant with His grace.
Look at it closely,
Read the words of love
He's written over, under,
Through and through.
Then give this loving God
Your heart, your love
So He can have a valentine
From you.

2/15/86

Love

A star's a shining symbol full,
A beating heart's a thimble full,
And words, when swift and nimble, fill
With love!

Love's more than an emotion.
It's a person,
It's an ocean.
It's a power set in motion
From above!

You can feel it, you can taste it,
You can swim in it
Or waste it.
Take it slowly or in haste
It still is love.

You can hurt it, you can spurn it,
Scourge it, crucify it, burn it,
But there's no way you can turn it
Off. So, love!

9/20/78

Cleansing

Snow covers everything,
Makes it all white and pure,
But when it melts,
We must again endure
The sight of all the ashes, leaves,
Dead grass, old weeds,
Decay and mess and dirt
Which winter hid.

And yet, I would not want
The snow to stay
\nd never go away.
Without the thawing
And the stark revealing
Of all that still needs
Cleaning up and healing,
Spring could not come.
The flowers would not bloom.
The birds would still be dumb.

Lord, make me brave enough
To be
Open
To Your great warming, healing light,
That by it, I may see
My life's debris
And let You clean me up
And make me right.

2/23/94

Seasons of Myself

Sometimes I am as young as spring
With new life peeking through,
With tender feelings blossoming
And reaching out to you.

Sometimes I am as old as old,
Everything frozen from the cold.
I huddle within myself and fold
Silence around me like a mold.

3/6/94

Doubt

Our world is muffled in moisture.
All the familiar shapes and sounds
Of view and trees
And barn roof and the road
Have vanished,
Shrouded in silence.
This gray mysterious presence
Has risen out of the wet leaves
And the mud and the melting snow
And wrapped within itself
The coming of spring.
I no longer believe
In the red wings and the pussy willows.
Was there once sunshine?
Was there really a robin?

3/23/79

Returning

Eden, for us,
Lies hedged about with thorn.
The beauty of its secret garden
Sleeps.

Deep in our memory
We know that distant dawn,
For we were there, became,
Were named and learned to name.

Today, we search the world,
The moons beyond the world
And worlds within ourselves,
Impenetrable and immense,
Seeking the garden we once knew
And our lost innocence.

2/19/86

New Horizons

Since I was always told
That grass was green,
I didn't think
(Until my own eyes saw)
That grass was pink.

There was this fringe of grass
Beside the walk,
Each slender stalk
Feathered with palest rose.

Now I am not so sure
That those who've known
All about grass
But only seen it mown
Can limit it for me.

If grass is pink,
Then grass contains
Such unimagined possibility.

7/2/87

Unicorns

Will we see unicorns again?
Is God preparing us through myth
For some lost place and time
Where we encounter the sublime?

There was a moment at the beach
And once, walking through new-blown snow,
A sense of magic just beyond my reach.
Was it the distant sound
Of silver hooves, impatient on the ground?

Will we see unicorns again?
Oh, Father, keep my heart from going blind
So, when the golden horns gleam in the air,
I will be sensitive enough to know
The unicorns are there.

1/30/81

Wade Collection

Fumbling within the wardrobes of my mind,
I find only black wood
And Lewis's old coat.
Perhaps if I were a child again,
I could dissolve through the back of my thoughts
And be gone
Into the pines and the snow
With Timnus, the fawn.
But all of the practical years
And my fears
Have grown like a thicket of thorns
While my spirit sleeps.
Oh, prince of our peace,
Find me and kiss me awake
And lead me back to Narnia
For Heaven's sake.

4/1/81

Forward Day by Day

Must you be always trudging,
Merely trudging?
Can you not hear the silver trumpets call?
These years are meant for blessing.
Don't go grudging
Along the road decreed for you above.
Rather with high and happy heart,
With singing,
With banners flying
Go upon your way.
Know in your heart
That every step is bringing
You closer
To that final glorious day!

8/13/89

Harbinger

As dainty and demure as nuns
Serenely coifed in slate and white,
The juncos have been faithful
Through the snow.
Suddenly,
All is movement and music.
A shimmer of shaken silver
Falls from the maples.
The bushes ring
With a myriad tiny bells.
Rejoice, my winter-weary heart!
It is the sound of spring.

3/10/79

Come Sweet Spring

I can remember spring
When I was young,
My heart flung blossom-wide
Before the sun.
Spring!
Will it warm me still
As I grow old?
Will I still thrill
To the first blue-veined crocus,
The first daffodil?
Try me, and see, sweet spring!
Come soon, be bold!

3/31/92

Epitaph

I hope it will be said
When I am dead,
"She wrote good poems
And she made good bread."

But let it not be said
Till I am dead.
To say it now
Would surely turn my head.

1/23/78